NEW LAKE CHURCH HISTORICAL SKETCH

Order this book online at www.trafford.com
or email orders@trafford.com

Most Trafford titles are also available at major online book retailers.

Print information available on the last page.

ISBN: 978-1-4907-6825-0 (sc)
ISBN: 978-1-4907-6824-3 (hc)
ISBN: 978-1-4907-6826-7 (e)

Library of Congress Control Number: 2015920958

Trafford rev. 07/18/2017

 www.trafford.com

North America & international
toll-free: 1 888 232 4444 (USA & Canada)
fax: 812 355 4082

PREFACE

This historical sketch of New Lake Church of Christ (Holiness) U.S.A., Jackson, MS, is a bird's eye view of the worship, ministry and activity of this local congregation and its effect in the community, in this geographic locality and in the District, Diocese and National Convention.

It also reveals the impact of the Christian life on individuals and their daily contacts. We pray that this document inspires present and future generations.

Disclaimer: The information in this book is a compilation of memories and interviews from current and past members of New Lake Church. Although the compiler and editors have made every effort to ensure that the information in this book is correct at this writing, due to deaths of key people, the changes in administration, and lost of documents through the years, the stories and names may be inconclusive. The compiler and editors hereby disclaim any liability to any party for any loss, damage or disruption caused by errors or omissions, whether such errors or omissions result from negligence, accident or any other cause.

DEDICATION

To the memory of the late
Joe D. King, Pastor

New Lake Church of Christ (Holiness) U.S.A.
1917 ~ 1946

Dedicatory Statement

This historical sketch of New Lake Church of Christ (Holiness) USA is dedicated to Elder J. D. King, one of the most effective, visionary pastors who ever served at the church. He pastored New Lake from 1917 to 1946 (29 years). During that time the church building was renovated, and we were in the planning stages of rebuilding when he passed away. During his tenure, 87 members were baptized and approximately 44 others joined the church. Elder King was a very gifted preacher and a beloved pastor. He set the pattern of spiritual steadfastness and brotherly love in the congregation and in the community. He pastored us longer than anyone else to date. Elder King was an inspiration to those of us who grew up under his pastorate. He made many sacrifices and showed much Christian concern for the flock. *The compiler chose to dedicate this history to his memory because of his longevity, and love for the congregation.*

ACKNOWLEDGEMENTS

Scripture references are from the Holy Bible, King James Version, unless otherwise indicated. We would also like to acknowledge the resourcefulness of the Original Editing Committee which was composed of volunteers named herein.

ORIGINAL EDITING COMMITTEE

Sisters Mamie B. Crockett and Nancy Whitehead and Brother Herbert Irvin

CONTRIBUTING COMMITTEE MEMBERS

Brother Alveno N. Castilla
Brother Willenham Castilla
Sister Magolia A. Castilla
Sister Mamie Ballard Crockett
Sister Jessica Q. Eglin
Sister Earnestine Ephfrom
Brother Joe Andrew Ford
Brother Herbert Irvin
Sister Jannie Ballard Johnson
Elder Lem Johnson
Brother Robert E. Myles
Sister Rubye B. Myles
Sister Sandrea J. Myles
Sister Mary Etta Myles Sutton
Sister Nancy Whitehead
Sister Jessie M. Williams

Table of Contents

ABOUT THE COMPILER

Willenham Castilla joined New Lake Church of Christ (Holiness) U.S.A. in 1937 at the age of 11. He has retained his membership there ever since. He is a graduate of Christ Missionary & Industrial College High School in Jackson, MS. He earned his Bachelor's of Science degree in Business Administration and Accounting from Jackson State University. He obtained his Master's in Theology from Christian Bible College and Seminary in Independence, MO. In 1995, the Department of Religious Education of Christ Missionary & Industrial College awarded him the honorary Doctor of Divinity degree at the National Convention of the Church of Christ (Holiness) U.S.A.

Dr. Castilla not only served on the local level as Sunday School Superintendent, HYPU President, Chairman of the Deacon Board, Director of Christian Education, Trustee and choir member but also served in the District as President of the Deacons and Wives Choir and Sunday School Convention President. In the Diocese, Castilla served as Treasurer for 38 years. He was the Executive Secretary of the National Education Trustee Board for several terms and Supervisor of the Diocese Deacons Relief Fund.

In the community, he has served in many capacities. He served as an Examiner in the Voting Rights Program for the U.S. Civil Service Commission in Alabama and Mississippi. He worked many years as a voting precinct manager in Madison County, MS. Castilla has been a Notary Public since 1960. In May 2002, Tougaloo College recognized him with a Meritorious Leadership Award..

Being an overseas veteran of World War II, Castilla continued his service with the Federal Government being employed with the Federal Postal Service. He became the first African-American promoted to supervisor in Jackson. MS. He retired as Postmaster (head of the facility) in Canton, MS.

A committed servant of God, Brother Castilla's motto is Philippians 4:8; ""Finally, brethren, whatsoever things are true, whatsoever things are honest, whatsoever things are just, whatsoever things are pure, whatsoever things are lovely, whatsoever things are of good report; if there be any virtue and if there be any praise, think on these things."" He is a native of Madison County, Mississippi. Castilla is, also, the oldest of four children born to Deacon Abraham and Sister Magolia Castilla. He was married to the late Sister Theresa Pearl Wright Castilla for 53 years. They are the parents of 9 children, 25 grandchildren and one great-grandchild.

FOREWORD

It has been noted throughout man's existence –– time brings about change. Many have argued the changes that have taken place over the course of history have been for the improvement of mankind. Others have argued those changes have been to the detriment of many societies.

I cannot definitively say which of two thoughts are most true. I can, however, offer a different thought.

Throughout history, there have always been persons who have been instrumental in creating, reviving or challenging the existing norms of their current social, religious and civic environments. These people or historic figures can be a source of shame to an entire community, much like Adolf Hitler; or these icons can be examples of honor and greatness in a community –– Martin Luther King, Jr. comes to mind.

Thankfully, these examples of how change and time can be a tragedy or an inspiration are not reserved for individuals with a first-hand account. Change and time was created in the hearts of individuals, like Dr. Willenham Castilla, the author of this work.

Dr. Castilla carries more than a passionate burden to record and preserve changes that have occurred throughout New Lake Church history. In this book, he and the historical committee have sought to capture and applaud the self- determination, religious devotion and singleness of mind of a people who south to create a community for the glory of God.

In the book, each page is an example of how time definitely brings change-but more importantly, how people during a course of time were agents of change.

Pastor, Elder Eddie L. Brown, Sr.

THE CORE VALUES OF THE CHURCH OF CHRIST (HOLINESS) USA

We are committed to being a community of worshippers

We are committed to a life of Holiness

We are committed to Evangelism

We are committed to Accountability and to pursing Excellence

We are committed to training Ministers and Lay Persons

DIVINE COMMISSION OF THE CHURCH OF CHRIST (HOLINESS) USA

The Church of Christ (Holiness) USA has a Divine commission to propagate the gospel throughout the world, seek the conversion of sinners, to reclaim backsliders, to encourage the sanctification of believers, to support divine healing, and to advance the truth of the return of our Lord and Savior Jesus Christ.

NEW LAKE CHURCH MISSION STATEMENT

Our mission is to be the church that loves God with all our hearts, minds, and strength; to go with unconditional love, to reach the lost and the hurting with the gospel of Jesus Christ; and to make disciples and send them to the uttermost parts of the earth.

INTRODUCTION

This section provides a profile of a predominantly African American church that was a vital part of the Holiness Movement initiated by Bishop Charles Price Jones. You will discover through these abbreviated historical sketches that Bishop Jones was effectively pastoring at the Mount Helm Baptist Church in Jackson, MS when he saw a need to live holy and to lead his congregation in doing the same. This section leads us through some valleys and mountains in the process of growing a denomination that was initiated by a black man in Jackson, Mississippi during the latter years of Reconstruction.

ORIGIN AND DEVELOPMENT

The CHURCH OF CHRIST (HOLINESS) U.S.A. had its beginning during the era of the ""Holiness Movement"" in the United States.

The DIVINE COMMAND to call holiness convocation was given to the late Bishop and later named Elder, Charles Price James in 1896. The first convention was held June 6, 1897. The main features of that first convention were: bible study, praying in and for the Holy Spirit, testimonies, as well as, preaching and singing.

Elder Charles Price Jones, DD, LL, D (C.P. Jones) was the founder, president and lifetime Senior Bishop of the Church of Christ (Holiness) U.S.A. The ""Holiness Movement"" –– as it is called, emphasized that the Christian lifestyle should exemplify Christ and show that ""God hath called His church unto Holiness"" (2 Corinthians 4:7; Hebrews 12:14). The movement was entirely inter-denominational at the time.

However, the mission was misunderstood. Historically, when people misunderstand something, they fear and fight. So the proponents of the movement were persecuted and eventually driven out of the various church bodies. This persecution caused us to build another sect and our own church houses, which was not the original aim and desire.

NEW LOCATION

Elder Thomas Sanders was one of the close associates of Bishop C.P. Jones. Elder Sanders was pastor of Hope Spring Missionary Baptist Church on Livingston Road. When he and his parishioners were put out of Hope Springs, they bought an acre of land where New Lake Church is presently located. In 1899 the people first met in a brush arbor that provided temporary shelter. In 1903, the first church house was erected. The contractor was a Herbert Hicks, who joined the church after he constructed the building. Hope Springs was commonly called The Lake Church because of a lake which was nearby. So when some of the members came to the new location, they called it New Lake Church.

THIS IS A DRAFT OF THE FIRST NEW LAKE CHURCH BUILDING.

NEW LAKE CHURCH SECOND BUILDING

Charter Members

BROTHERS

Frank Berry
Pete Patrick
Thomas Roach
Eddie Silas
Pete Silas

SISTERS

India Berry
Elmira Ballard Castilla
Ella Commander
Emma Jones
Nancy McCoy
Laura Patrick
Sarah Roach
Ada Warren

Early Pioneers and Decendents

Frank Berry
India Berry
Elmira Ballard Castilla
Ella Commander
Elnora V. Ellis
Emma Jones
Mary Collins Myles
Henry Patrick

Laura Patrick
Nancy McCoy
Sarah Roach
Thomas Roach
Eddie Silas
Pete Silas
Ada Warren
Ida Williams

Other Early Members

Willie Ballard
Levora Vincent Ford
Ruth Hicks Ford
Herbert Hicks

Fannie Horton
Armella McNair Myles
(Mrs.) Michael-Turner
Daisy Turner

PROGRESS THROUGH THE YEARS

After Elder Sanders passed away, Bishop, (then Elder) J.L.I. Conic served as Interim Pastor. In 1917, a young preacher, originally from Hazlehurst, MS, named Joe D. King began his passionate leadership here at New Lake Church for a duration of 29 years. During his tenure, the church building was remodeled. He passed away in 1946 while funds were being raised to build a new edifice.

In 1947, Bishop, then Elder Clifton Goodloe, Sr. became our pastor. He provided leadership in the building of the new church. Elder Leo Butler was the pastor of this church for a short time. Then Elder L.P. Camper came and led in making several spiritual and material improvements before departing for a position in Chicago, Illinois.

Our sixth pastor was Elder William M. Jones from McComb, MS. He emphasized maintaining the church building and surrounding at its best. After his death, J.L.I. Graham was assigned to us as Pastor. Elder Graham had a special interest in the youth of the church. The next pastor, for a brief time, was Elder Edgar Calloway. From 1971 to 1982 Elder J.D. Washington served as Pastor, driving from Prentiss, MS. Bishop, (then Elder) Maurice D. Bingham, served in an Assistant Pastoral capacity. During those years, we moved from having worship service on two Sundays to having worship service on three Sundays. A few years later, we began having worship services every Sunday.

By that time, New Lake had become a service providing entity in the area. We housed a Head Start Center and subsequently, a center for Self-Help Training and Socialization for Handicapped Children, funded directly from the U.S. Department of Health, Education and Welfare. The center was the only one of its kind in the State for educating handicapped children. This educational outreach initiated by Deaconess Theresa Castilla was used as a model by the State of Mississippi. Structurally, we added a library, classrooms and obtained a water system to help accommodate the community service.

In 1983 Elder Clifton Montgomery was our next pastor. He left to go to another Diocese. Then Elder Thomas M. Jenkins, Sr. became our pastor. He came while we were in the process of planning the construction of the present edifice. In addition to completing the new construction, Elder Jenkins also led in the purchase of 34 acres of land in the nearby vicinity. We also began purchasing additional acreage around the church grounds. Elder Jenkins left the Church of Christ (Holiness) U.S.A. in January 2000. Many members of New Lake Church went with him.

Bishop Joseph R. Campbell, Sr. served as Interim Pastor from February 2000 until August 2001. Our next pastor, Elder Eddie L. Brown, Sr., was appointed September 2001. Under Elder Brown's leadership, membership has increased. All boards, auxiliaries and ministries are functioning well and all debt has been paid off.

New Lake Church owns about 40 acres of land in the Lakeover area of the City of Jackson. There are two parking lots and a church facility with plans to provide additional services to the surrounding community.

As Elder Brown states,

"The future is as bright as the promises of God."

NEW LAKE'S CURRENT CHURCH BUILDING

PASTORS
Through the years......

Elder Eddie L. Brown, Sr.

Elder Leo Butler

Elder Edgar Calloway

*Bishop Joseph R. Campbell, Jr.

Elder L. P. Camper

*Elder J.L.I. Conic

Elder Clifton Goodloe

Elder J. L. I. Graham

Elder Thomas M. Jenkins, D.D.

Elder William M. Jones

Elder Joe D. King (29 Years)

Elder Clifton Montgomery

Elder Thomas Sanders

Elder J.D. Washington

Served as an Interim Pastor

OTHER PREACHERS

Elder Aaron Ballard

Elder James (Jack) Ballard

Elder Nelson Ballard

Elder Maurice D. Bingham

Elder Willie Bingham

Elder Kerry Brown

Elder Quemardo M. Castilla

Elder W. Cortez Castilla

Minister Henry Coleman

Elder Robert Deloach

Minister James Ford

Elder Manual Greenfield

Minister Otis Harris

Elder David Horton

Elder David Johnson

Elder Lem Johnson

Minister David Jones

Minister V. David Kennebrew

Elder Gregory McGee

Elder Aaron McKanders

Elder Anderson Myles, Sr.

Elder Arlandis Powell

Elder Howard Rouson

Elder Daryl Thigpen

Minister Nathaniel Washington

Elder Ted Watkins

Minister Dan Wells

Minister James Young

DEACONS
Through the years......

Abraham Castilla

Alveno N. Castilla

Willenham Castilla

Quemardo M. Castilla

Sam Cobbins

Walter Crockett

Ronald Duffy

Erskine Forbes

Sidney Graves

Gregory Green

David Horton

Herbert Irvin

Alford Jackson

Anderson Myles, Jr.

Anderson Myles, Sr.

Henry Patrick

Curtis Proctor

Thomas Roach

Eddie Silas

Lamanous Simeons

Johnnie Stewart

*Thomas G. Sutton

Moses Turner

Edgar Williams

Willie Williams

* Watch care member

DEACONESSES
Through the years......

Lucille Ballard

Danyel Castilla

Theresa P. Castilla

Marlene Cline

Daisy Cobbins

Mamie B. Crockett

Earnestine Ephfrom

Ruth Ford

Lurlene Irvin

Idella Patrick

Mary Etta Myles Sutton

Virginia Silas

Patricia Vaughn

TRUSTEES
Through the years......

Lenard Brent

Alveno N. Castilla

Willenham Castilla

Sam Cobbins

Walter Crockett

Clarence Harris

Jamie Harris

Frank Hendricks

Curtis Johnson

Tony Jones

Ollie McClendon

Anderson Myles, Jr.

Robert E. Myles

Henry Patrick

Isadore W. Patrick

Arthur Speech

Cherrita Speech

Jack Thomas

Leon Thomas

Arthur Lee Turner

Edgar Williams

Jessie M. Williams

Lenard Brent

Portis Perkins

Kim Wade

BOARDS, AUXILLARIES & MINISTRIES (BAMS)

Through the years......

1. Brotherhood Ministries
2. Boy Scouts of America Troop
3. Children's Church
4. Christian Education and Discipleship Department
5. Compassionate Ministries and Benevolence Committee
6. Couples Ministry
7. Courtesy and Greeting Committee
8. Deacon Board
9. Deacon Relief Ministries
10. Deaconess Board
11. Evangelism Team
12. Finance and Budgetary Committee
13. Food Distribution Ministry
14. Food and Fellowship Committee
15. HYM (Holiness Youth Ministry)

    Formerly called the Holiness Young People's Union (HYPU)

16. Library/Etiquette Committee

17. Media Ministry
18. Nursery Committee
19. Nursing Home Ministry
20. Prison Ministry
21. Publicity and Public Relations Team
22. Music Ministry
    a. Children's Choir
    b. Inspirational Choir
    c. Male Chorus
    d. Praise Team
    e. Voices of Victory
    f. Youth Choir
23. Singles Ministry
24. Sunday School
25. Trustee Board
26. U.C.W.M. (United Christian Women's Ministry)
    a. Daughters of Esther
27. Ushers & Nurses Ministry
28. Van Ministry

Some Highlights of Activities
Through the years......

Sacred music, especially singing, has played a major role in the worship and programs at New Lake COCHUSA throughout its history.

Perhaps some of the musical inclination has been due to the overall glorious music in worship of the National Church Body all through history. The founder of the work, the Late Bishop C.P. Jones was a gifted, anointed and accomplished musician. He wrote and set to music more than a thousand songs and hymns. He provided his peers with a wide variety of sacred music.

Following this pattern, New Lake was one of the local churches that placed much emphasis on sacred music utilizing the choir, quartettes, soloist and other ensembles.

Some of the pianists and organist through the years have been: Sister Sally Thomas from Christ Temple, Brother J. C. Williams of Cynthia, Sister Agnes Bingham Nelson of Third Temple, Sister Loraine Hudson of Hyde Park M. B. Church, Brother Aaron Thompson of Cade Chapel M. B. Church, Sister Cornelia Whittaker, Brother Richard Jenkins, Brother W. Cortez Castilla, Brother Quemardo M. Castilla, Sister Henrene Patrick, Sister Jessie M. Castilla Williams, Sister Pearlie K. Barnes, Sister Ernestine Ephfrom, Sister Trenia Allen, Sister Maudell Silas Williams, Sister Cherritta Speech, Brother Cedric Hollis and Brother Brian Bell; all members of New Lake. Also, Brother Lee Campbell, Jr. plays the bass guitar. Some of the drummers have been Brothers Deon Buchanan, Jermaine Proctor, Gayland Sayles, and Michael Lloyd.

New Lake Church has participated in various worthwhile functions in the surrounding community. Our deacons were instrumental in providing transportation for families (especially children) during revivals, Daily Vacation Bible School and Bible Club meetings. The church has always been active in the District, diocese and National Convention.

Sister Magolia Jones Castilla served for several terms as a member of the standing finance committee of the Christian Women Willing Workers in the old Jackson and Terry District. Sister Armella McNair Myles was District Secretary of the Sunday School & Holiness Young People's Union convention for two terms. Sister Bettye L. Seaton-Jones Young served as local and district secretary of the Sunday School Department. Bother Willenham Castilla has served in several offices in the district, diocese and national convention including: District Sunday School

Missionary, HYPU Treasurer, Diocese Treasurer for the Parent Body, Executive Secretary of the National Education Trustee Board of Christ Missionary and Industrial College.

Sister Theresa P. Wright Castilla was president of the local CWWW for at least two terms. Sister Pearlie K. Myles Barnes was District Vice President of the Christian Women Willing Worker for several years. Willenham Cortez Castilla was Director of the High School Chorus at C.M. & I College. Later, he became the Minister of Music for the national convention. Sam Cobbins served several terms as Chairman of the National Education-Trustee Board of the COCHUSA. Sister Jannie Ballard Johnson was a member of New Lake when she was Elected National Missionary of the Church of Christ (Holiness) U.S.A.

New Lake has had several young people to participate in the S.S. & HYPU Congress on each level. On the national level, Earnestine Tate, Mary D. Castilla, Fonya Crockett, Andrealene Myles and Sharon Myles were some of the oratorical contestants. New Lake has had participants in the congress Bible Bowls and Bible Quizzes nearly every year. Quemardo Castilla was our music contestant who was a winner in the National Congress. Pastor, Elder Eddie L. Brown, Sr., serves as secretary of the Ordination Commission of the South Central Diocese. He also serves as Vice Chairman of the Evangelism Committee of the National Convention.

SOME FAMILY CONTRIBUTIONS AND/OR ACTIVITIES

We owe much of the heritage, success and progress in God's work to the faithfulness of some of the members of this congregation through the years. Not all are listed here, but they are the ones recalled. Others are listed in the Lamb's Book of Life.

Deacon Henry Patrick was very loyal and dutiful. For several years, he worked as a night watchman at the New Capitol Building and other places. Yet, he would attend the worship and other meetings at New Lake Church, even though he would be ever so sleepy. He was the second person to be chairman of the Deacon Board.

Deacon Patrick's wife was very active in the church. She was Sister Idella Patrick. Her brother, Dr. Harry Jones, was a Foreign Missionary who served in Africa the major part of his life. He loved the mission field!

Deacon Henry and Sister Idell Patrick have three children who were members of New Lake. They were Isadoree Walter, Earl Alphonse and Henrene Patrick. Isadore and his wife, Estelene (Dot) has a daughter, Dorothy Ann and a son Isadore, Jr., Attorney-at- law.

The first person to be the chairman of the Deacon Board was Brother Eddie Silas. Deacon Silas, on several occasions, would walk about five miles to visit Deacon Abraham Castilla just to talk about how they could do things to improve the deacon board and the church operations. Brother and Sister Silas had some sons; namely, Charlie, Chris and Joel. They also had daughters. They were Laura and Annie (Pises). Sister Virginia Silas, wife of Deacon Eddie, served as president of the local CWWW.

Sister Elmira Ballard Castilla had four brothers. Three of them were preachers. Brother Willie (Willis) Ballard was not a preacher. Her other brothers were: Elder James (Jack) Ballard, Elder Nelson Ballard and Elder Aaron Ballard.

Brother Willie's children were: Catherine, Willie, Jr., Eddie, Lee Edward, Albert, Earnest and Elder James (Jack) Ballard. Elder James Ballard was one of the associate ministers at New Lake Church. He and two of the deacons baptized new members. His children were: Johnny Ballard who died in his young adulthood; Georgia Ballard Guice, Sarah Ballard Guice (two sisters married two brothers, Willie and Earnest Guice); Eliza Ballard Tate (John).

Elder James (Jack) Ballard's grandchildren: Willie Mae Seaton (Tobe), Benny Guice (Myrtis Ford), Sarah Bell Guice, John L. Guice, Ernestine Guice Marshall, J.B. Guice and Doris Guice.

Great grandchildren of Elder James Ballard: Rufus Seaton, Betty Lee Seaton-Jones –– F. Young, Benny's son and daughter, Eliza Tate's children. Ernestine Tate Ephfrom is still very active at New Lake Church.

Elder Nelson Ballard established the Ballard Chapel Church and Spring Hill School in Madison County, MS. His son and daughters were: James, Percy, Seth, Jannie, Bessie, Celeste, Charles Price and Sylvester Ballard. His wife was the former Jannie McClaurin. His grandchildren: Percy, Jr., Geraldine, Seth, Jr., (Augusta), Rosa Mae Townsend, Monroe (Joeann), Jannie (Elder Lem Johnson), Daisy (Dr. Sam Cobbins), Mamie (Dr. Walter L. Crockett), Samuel (Florice) and Reverend Sylvester (Evelyn), Maceo, Charles, Jr., James, Dorothy and Edwina. Sister Elmira Ballard Castilla's youngest brother, Elder Aaron Ballard, pastored in Leland, MS and other places in the Greenville District. He and his wife, Annie and some of their children moved to Detroit, MI, then later to Los

Angeles, CA. There, he founded Second Temple COCHUSA in Los Angeles. Their children were: Willenham, Daniel, Aaron, Jr. and Samuel Ballard; and Bessie, Emily Ballard, Maggie Ballard Farmer, Odessa Ballard Plummer, Annie Bell Ballard Thrash and Gussie Ballard.

Elder James (Jack) Ballard has a grandson preaching. He is Reverend Johnny Tate, Jr., son of Sister Eliza Tate. Elder Nelson Ballard has a grandson who is a preacher, Reverend Sylvester Ballard.

He also has great grandsons preaching. They are Prentiss Ballard, son of Samuel and Florice Ballard and Lemzel Johnson, son of Elder Lem and Jannie Ballard Johnson.

Elder Aaron Ballard, Sr.'s son, Samuel was also a preacher. Pastor Dr. John Plummer, Jr. was his grandson. Dr. Plummer was the founder and pastor of New Testament COCHUSA in Los Angeles, CA. His son, Aaron, Jr. has a son who is a preacher.

Sister Elmira Ballard Castilla of New Lake Church has a grandson who is a minister of gospel, Nelson Castilla of Washington, DC. She has five grandsons who are ministers of the gospel in the COCHUSA, namely: Elder W. Cortez Castilla of Jackson, MS, Elder Vonzell Castilla of Atlanta, GA, Elder Don C. Williams of Baton Rouge, LA, Minister Robert R. Williams of Gary, IN and Elder Quemardo M. Castilla of Jackson, MS. Her great-great-grandsons in the gospel ministry are: Ministers Daniel E. Kennebrew and Minister V. David Kennebrew of Houston, TX and Jackson, MS, respectively.

Deacon Moses Turner and wife, Daisy had no children. He had a brother, Arthur Lee and a sister Ida Mae Turner Keys who served as clerk of our church for several years. A young man named Peter Turner was living with Deacon Moses Turner for a while. He must have been a close family relative.

It is not recalled that Deacon Earskine Forbes had any family members at New Lake Church. Deacon Willie Williams (some people called him ""Will Moore"") and his wife, Josephine Towers-Moore had no children.

Brother Abraham Castilla was a deacon. He especially loved music and was a member of the choir. A well-recognized tenor singer, he served several terms as church treasurer and was a Sunday school teacher. His wife was Sister Magolia Jones Castilla. Their children: Willenham Castilla, Julia Abranese Castilla Hicks, Jessie Magolia Castilla Williams and Nelson Castilla. Information was given earlier about the activities of Willenham. Julia Abranese served as secretary in the local and in the District Sunday School and HYPU. She also sang with her sister, Jessie Magolia at the piano. Nelson became a trained vocalist.

Deacon Vivian H. Williams transferred his membership from White Rock M. B. Church to New Lake circa the 1940s. His mother, Sister Ella Williams was already a member here. His wife and five youngest children later became members of New Lake. They were: Sister Geneva Hulett Williams, Henry Thomas (H.T.), Robert Lee, James, Delores and Edna. Their three older children were already members of Cynthia COCHUSA and other churches. They were Eleanor, Margaret and John Cole (J.C.).

In 1953, Brother Robert Lee Williams and Sister Jessie Magolia Castilla Williams were active members of New Lake Church of Christ (Holiness) USA before migrating to Newark, New Jersey. After 44 years, Brother Robert and Sister Jessie Williams returned to Jackson, MS, (1997) and reunited with the New Lake Church family.

Having returned at a slightly turbulent time in New Lake Church's history, Brother and Sister Williams volunteered their services where needed. The couple worked in the maintenance and lawn services of New Lake. During that time, Brother Williams installed the first timer for exterior lights, set up flower beds, planted two paring apple trees and repaired the pew pockets in the church. He was later elected as a trustee at New Lake. Brother Robert L. Williams continued to serve at New Lake Church until the time of his death on March 12, 2009. His volunteer work remains as a positive memory. The Williams also served in the church in Gary, IN for many years.

During the latter part of the era of the original deacons came Deacon George Kelley, who transferred his membership from Christ Temple at Tougaloo. He was a contractor and very efficiently added space to our church building for a fellowship hall and Head Start facility.

Sister Pearlie K Barnes was a certified teacher, counselor, administrator, CEO of a day care center and foster care mother. Her son, Kenneth Barnes, and daughters Renee and Carolyn Barnes grew up at New Lake. All participated in the choir and youth activities. Renee and her two children (Kobi and Khalil) are still active members at New Lake. Sis. Barnes is also responsible for bringing the Parker grandchildren to New Lake (Johnny, Beverli, Cheryl, John, Stan, Howard, Jr., Christopher, Denetta and Darrell Parker). Beverli Parker Garner and her husband became members for a while, and Beverli served as a children's church worker. Charlie Parker married Sonya Garner and she joined New Lake along with her two children (Bobby and Quindel).

It is noteworthy to mention that during the mid to late 1980's, New Lake was blessed to experience an influx of strong new recruits who had no previous affiliation with COCHUSA, but who became committed stalwart members. Several of these persons are either still at New Lake or affiliated with COCHUSA. Some of the people in this category that we can recall include Nancy Whitehead (now the New Lake financial secretary). Herbert Irvin (now a deacon and member of several other key boards and committees). Lurlean Irvin (now a deaconess). Joan Straughter, Christine Ross (who married Reginald Castilla after coming to New Lake). Crystal Tate, Kerry Brown (who became an ordained minister in COCHUSA and served many years before his untimely death).

Helen Bennett was recruited to New Lake by Joan Straughter who was an active missionary and church worker. Helen grew spiritually and fervently. She became church clerk in 2000, and remained at New Lake when the church was dividing between the current church and the membership that followed Rev. Thomas Jenkins, She was a Sunday School teacher and a church greeter. She was woman of the year in 2000, and served as district president of the United Women Ministries for several terms.

Dr. Sam Cobbins, Professor at Jackson State University served as church treasurer, as chair of the trustee board of New Lake for many years and as chair of the board for the program for handicapped children initiated by Sis. Theresa Castilla. Sister Daisy Ballard Cobbins, Sam's wife, was a certified elementary teacher. She compiled and edited two documents that helped with church growth and maintaining membership: (1) A Practical Guide for Evangelism (1985), published by the New Lake Church Evangelism Team and (2) Membership Handbook (1985, Revised, 1993), published by New Lake Church and Pastor, Thomas Melvin Jenkins. She served as coach for the Bible Bowl during the late 1970's and 1980's. Holiness Young People's, HYPU, won consecutive annual awards for New Lake. Sister Raquel Cobbins Marion, Sam's and Daisy daughter grew up at New Lake. She served as Sunday School secretary, choir member and later traveled with the WORD singing group out of Memphis. Their son, Sam Bradford Cobbins was instrumental in getting young people involved in Scripture-based drama at New Lake. He sang in the choir and participated in HYPU. Bradford later married Jacqueline (Jackie). She joined New Lake and has served faithfully on the Hospitality Committee, as Sunday school teacher and as a church usher.

Sister Georgia Guice was a very active member. She served as a faithful usher and Sunday school member. Her daughter, Sister Willie Mae Guice Seaton was a great Sunday school teacher, and usher, and president of the Pastor"s Aide Club for many years. Her children: Rufus Seaton, Clarence and Betty Seaton Young grew up at New Lake. Rufus and Betty served in various capacities, but most memorable was that Rufus became A Sunday school superintendent and Betty was the secretary for several years. Tony Jones, the son of Betty and grandson of Sis. Georgia Guice is still a member at New Lake. He is a Trustee Board Member.

Dr. Walter L Crockett joined New Lake Church after marrying Sister Mamie Ballard. During his tenure at New Lake, Bro. Crockett has served as Sunday school superintendent, trustee, deacon, and Chairman of the deacon board. As Sunday school superintendent, he initiated the first van ministry for Sunday school and youth retreat during the Christmas holidays. For almost twenty years, he co-chaired with his wife the Youth Department that supervised all children and youth ministries of the church. Dr. Mamie Ballard Crockett has served as chair of the deaconess board for thirty plus years, initiated children church at New Lake during the 1970"s and still serves as coordinator of children's church. She has participated in Sunday school CWWW and UCWM (women ministry) on local, district and national levels. She was selected as Woman of the year in 2006 by COCHUSA . The Crocketts have four children who were nurtured by family and New Lake Church (Fonya C Scott (Science teacher), Walter L Jr (Instructor of Marketing and Business), Robert S (Podiatric Medical Doctor), and Crysenthia C Stewart (Administrator for Social Security). Fonya was secretary for the Sunday school and served as HYPU president for several years. Walter, Jr. participated in Sunday school, choir and the drama club. Robert Seth participated in Sunday school and church activities. Crysenthia served as secretary for the Sunday school until after college graduation when her career moved her to Florida.

Bro. Arthur Speech worked with the brotherhood, served as a trustee and instructor in children's church. Sis. Cherrita Speech worked as Church Music Coordinator, trustee and Sunday school teacher of New Lake. She currently serve as Children's music director for diocese and National music workshop.

Deacon A. M. Myles Jr., son of Elder Anderson Myles, was a choir member, served as Superintendent of Sunday School and was a trustee during the completion of the present structure.

Other deacons who came served mostly during the administration of Pastor Thomas M. Jenkins and left with him when he left the COCHUSA. Among them were: Deacons Ronald Duffy, Lamaneas Simeons, Gregory Green, and Alford Jackson. Deacons Otis Harris and David Horton also served as deacons under Elder Thomas Jenkins' leadership, but were called to the ministry and left prior to Elder Jenkins leaving.

Deacons ordained under the leadership of Pastor Eddie L. Brown are Deacons Curtis Proctor, Quemardo M. Castilla, Michael Anderson and Centron Lenoir. Also, two other deacons have transferred into our congregation, namely: Deacons Thomas G. Sutton and Johnny Stewart from Christ Temple, Jackson, MS and St. Peter, Hazlehurst, MS respectively.

HISTORICAL SKETCH OF PASTORS

Elder Thomas Sanders, Founder, who came from Hope Springs Missionary Baptist Church, where he and several followers had been put out of the Baptist Church. He was a close associate of Senior Bishop Charles Price Jones. He pastored New Lake until his death.

Bishop (then Elder) J. L. I. Conic served as pastor on an interim basis. In 1917, Elder Joe D. King of Hazlehurst, MS, became a pastor. Later, he moved to Jackson. He pastored New Lake for 29 years. Elder King was known for many evangelistic practices. He spent most of his time reading the Holy Bible and could quote scripture verbatim. He was paper hanger by trade, but spent most to his time studying the Word. The collection and church income ranged from monetary offerings to vegetables raised on various farms of members. He rode the bus to visit members in their homes, especially to see the sick and shut-ins. Everyone loved and respected him-both young and old. Elder J. D. King became very ill and died an untimely death in 1946.

Next, Elder (later Bishop) Clifton Goodloe, Sr. came as pastor. During his administration a new edifice was quickly built. Chairman of the trustee board, Brother Leon Thomas was the general contractor. Elder Goodloe resigned to accept a pastorate in Louisiana where he became Diocese Overseer. Later he became presiding Bishop of the Southwestern Diocese.

Elder Leo Butler served well for a short time.

Elder L.P. Camper was the next pastor. Young, energetic and courageous, he led us in making improvements including a running water system, baptized three converts, stepped up the Sunday School to opening at 9:30 a.m. and left on his own accord.
He moved to Chicago for a while.

Our sixth pastor was Elder William M. Jones of McComb, MS. He had been a railroad employee, so he had special train transportation. A warm hearted man of understanding and leadership ability, his motto was: ""keep the church, its surroundings and belonging at their best."" During his administration we brought a new piano, a new lawn mower and accepted five new converts. All auxiliaries were functioning well when he went to eternal rest.

Elder J.L.I. Graham had been the pastor of Philadelphia Baptist Church in Chicago, IL. When he moved to Jackson, MS he joined the Church of Christ (Holiness USA. He became the next pastor of New Lake. He was the son of the Elder J.E. Graham who became the next pastor of New Lake. He was the son of the Elder J.E. Graham who had transferred his membership

to the COCHUSA in his latter years. Elder J.L.I. Graham preached short, but deep and soul stirring sermons. He left New Lake to pastor at Cynthia Church, where his father had pastored before he passed away.
Meanwhile, Elder Edgar Calloway, a young pastor came to us from Cynthia Church; however, his tenure was limited, eventually, he became a pastor of a Baptist church across town.

Elder J. D. Washington was appointed pastor of New Lake by Bishop A.J. Torrey in 1971. Elder Washington commuted from Prentiss, MS. This was during the period of time when church services moved up from two Sundays to three Sundays per month. Elder Washington was very strong on staff-type administration in the operation of the local church. He often referred to the deacons and officers of the church as his ""cabinet."" Even though he was driving from out of town and his health was failing, Elder Washington carried on a strong leadership.

Then, came Elder Clifton Montgomery. Now, again, here was a pastor who lived in the city of Jackson. He was a relatively young man with modern ideas and appealed to young people. But he soon left us to accept a position in another state.

The next pastor was Elder Thomas Melvin Jenkins. He was one of the sons of the late, great, Elder Willie Jenkins, a well-known pastor and District Chairman in the Jackson area. Elder Thomas M. Jenkins had a very notable following and was very influential in church and business affairs. After a few years with us, our membership increased from about 40 members to over 500 members. The number of worship services increased to two per Sunday. We began extensive ministries and Evangelism Training using the Evangelism Manual developed by New Lake. However, there occurred factions and group patterns within the congregation. Then suddenly, in January 2000 Elder Jenkins resigned as pastor, left the denomination, split the congregation and carried more than two-thirds of the members with him.

Consequently, New Lake Church had to recover from a devastating set back. In our effort to hold the local church together, Bishop Joseph R. Campbell came and took charge as interim pastor for about 18 months while we rebuilt our fellowship.

However, we found ourselves on the move and progressing as we began rebuilding relationships and developing spiritually, numerically, and financially. Elder Eddie L. Brown was appointed as new pastor in September 2001.

Elder Brown made tremendous progress in bringing the church back from the brink of disaster. Examples of this progress are shown through our reports to the District at the end of the church fiscal year 2009/2010.

		FIRST MONTH	SECOND MONTH	THIRD MONTH	QUARTERLY TOTAL
NAME OF CURCH OR DISTRICT	New Lake				
REPORTING PERIOD: QUARTER	4th I YEAR I 2009/2010				
CONTACT PERSON (FOR QUESTIONS) Nancy Whitehead 601953-8491					
A.	CHURCH RECEIPTS (ROUND OFF IN DOLLARS)				
1	Church Tithes & Offerings (Only)	$ 14,834.00	$ 14,741.51	$ 15,841.31	$ 45,416.82
2	General Missions Offerings	$ 126.00	$ 135.20	$ 139.00	$ 400.20
3	Capitol Projects and/or Building Fund	$	$		$
4	Church Rental Income (Building Rental, Interest, Etc.)				
5	All Other Church Receipts (Gifts, Contributions and Donations)	$ 240.00	$ 112.00	$ 52.00	$ 404.00
6	Sunday School (SS) & HYM	$ 351.10	$ 310.46	$ 318.03	$ 979.59
7	United Christian Women Ministry (UCWM)	$	$	$	$
8	Brotherhood Ministry (NBM)				
9	All Other Receipts and Revenues (Individuals, Auxiliaries/Committees or Groups)				
10	TOTAL PERCENTAGED REVENUE (TOTAL LINE 2 THROUGH LINE10) I	$ 15,551.10	$ 15,299.17	$ 16,350.34	$ 47,200.61
	AMOUNT THAT IS DUE BASED ON 5 PERSENT (MONTHLY TOTAL- LINE 11 TIMES .05)				$ 2,360.00
	AMOUNT THAT IS DUE BASED ON 5 PERSENT (MONTHLY TOTAL- LINE 11 TIMES .05)				$ 2,360.00
	TOTAL DUE DISTRICT BASED ON ADDING 5 ANFD 5 PERCENT				$ 4,720.00
	Non-Percentaged Reveune (Exclusions):				
11	Mission Funds for Earmarked Activity: (e.g. Youth Activity, Naomi Doles, Fund not retained)	$ 1,661.00	$ 45.00	$ 575.00	$ 2,281.00
12	Funds from Loans	$			
13	Pastor1s Anniversary				
14	Speakers Love Offerings - Raisedfor Guest Speaker	$			
15	Specific Contributions (Endowments, Grants, Gifts from Deceased members or friends)	$			
16	Day Care Activity (Not legally Separated From The Church)	$			
17	Affiliated 501-3c Entity	$			

18	Rental Property Income (Other Than The Church Building)	$			$
19	All other Extraordinary Exclusions (Must be pre-Approved by the Presiding Bishop)	$			$
20	Total Non-Percentaged Revenue (TOTAL LINE 14 THROUGH LINE 24)	$ 1,661.00	$ 45.00	$ 575.00	$ 2,281.00
21	Total Income for Church or District (LINE 11PLUS LINE 25)				
B.	CHURCH EXPEDENTITURES (ROUND OFFIN DOLLARS)				
22	Pastor's Support	$ 3,231.00	$ 3,231.00	$ 4,189.00	$ 10,651.00
23	Church Salaries	$ 3,994.00	$ 3,048.00	$ 3,699.00	$ 10,741.00
24	Mission and Benevolence	$ 100.00	$ 125.00	$ 255.00	$ 580.00
25	Interest Expense	$	$	$	$
26	Current Operating Expenses (Utilities, Etc.)	$ 6,190.00	$ 3,096.00	$ 4,379.00	$ 13,665.00
27	Building Equipment/Other Assets	$	$	$	$
28	Capita I Projects	$	$	$	
29	Rental Property Expense	$	$	$	
30	Mortgage Loan Annual Repayments	$	$	$	
31	Other Loans Annual Repayments	$	$	$	
32	Other Church Expenditures	$ 5,924.00	$	$ 5,924.00	$ 5,924.00
33	TOTAL CHURCH EXPENDITURES (TOTAL LINE 28 THROUGH LINE 39)	$ 19,539.00	$ 9,500.00	$ 12,522.00	$ 41,561.00
C.	*REPORT ANNUAL AMOUNTS ON FOURTH QUARTER REPORT FOR CONVENTION YEARLINES 34-41*				
34	Casn Bala nee				$ 80,795.00
35	Value of church Property				$ 800,000.00
36	Value of Other Real Estate/ Parsonage				$ 152,000.00
37	Value of Other Assets - Van etc				$ 30,000.00
38	TOTAL CHURCH ASSETS (TOTAL LINE 44 THROUGH LINE 48)				$ 1,062,795.00
D.	CHURCH LIABILITIES (ROUND OFF TO DOLLARS)				

39	Real Estate Loan Balance		
40	Car/Bus Loans		
41	Balance of other Loans		
42	TOTAL CHURCH LIABILITIES (TOTAL LINE 52 THROUGH LINE 55)		

TRUSTEES
Through the years......

Recalled memories: Brother Edgar Williams, who also served as sexton, was a trustee. Brother Isadore Patrick who seemed to have a special love for the upkeep of the building; Brother Leon Thomas a building contractor, served on a regular basis in the maintenance of the premises. Brother A. M. Myles, Jr. and Brother Alveno Castilla played a major role in working with the contractor in the construction of our present edifice. Dr. Sam Cobbins, the next trustee chairman, an Industrial Arts Instructor, offered technical advice. Dr. Curtis Johnson, at the time of this writing, is the chairman of the trustee board. Others serving were and are: Brothers Robert E. Myles, Robert L. Williams, Herbert Irvin, Curtis Proctor, Leonard Brent, Donald Vaughan, Tony Jones, Ollie McClendon, Frank Hendricks, Portis Perkins, Kim Wade, Sisters Jessie M. Williams and Cherrita Speech.

DEACONESS BOARDS

The activities of the Deaconess Boards during early years were limited to preparing the Lord's Supper, making ready for baptizing and helping potential, as well as, new members get acquainted with church procedures. In more recent times, the deaconesses have also taken on the role of helping the young women become more active in outreach and in-reach, as well as, doing altar work. Former and current board members are: Sister Daisy Ballard Cobbins, Mamie Ballard Crockett, Lucille Ballard Austin, Theresa P Wright Castilla, Earnestine Tate Ephfrom, Mary Etta Myles Sutton, Lurlene Irvin, Marlene Cline, Danyel Castilla, Patricia Vaughn and Carmen Castilla.

SUNDAY SCHOOL & HOLINESS YOUTH MINISTRIES (HYM)
Historical Sketch

During the 1930s, Brother Moses Turner was Superintendent of Sunday School at New Lake. After he left the Jackson area for a while, several other men served. But the next longest serving superintendent was Brother Vivian H. Williams. During that time, he conceived and projected the idea of establishing a library for the youth.
Sister Elnora V. Ellis kept the Sunday school reminded about getting the library started. The Seth and Lucille Ballard family provided furnishing for

it. The Myles family also made contributions. When the first addition was made to the ""little white"" church, a room for the library was included.

The Sunday school was the liveliest part of New Lake Church during the late 1940s, 1950s and the early 1960s. Brother Willenham Castilla was superintendent for those years. Brother Robert Earl Myles served as superintendent of the Sunday school in 1954-1955. Other superintendents were Brothers Rufus Seaton, Gabriel Robinson, Walter Crockett, Jim Owens and Gregory Green. The HYPU (as it was called then) was the fun part of the church, as well as, the training auxiliary for youth, young adults and parents.

Some of the active youth and young adults remembered are: Aaron and Maude Lee McKanders, the grandchildren of Sister Fannie Horton; Ola Mae Williams, granddaughter of Brother Edgar and Sister Ida Williams; Cornelia and Elizabeth Williams, daughters of Edger Williams; Betty McGowan Robinson, also their granddaughter. Later Betty's children, Angela and Gabriel Robinson engaged religious growth and development of early childhood at New Lake Church. Under Elder Thomas Jenkins' tenure a Youth Department was developed and Brother Walter and Sister Mamie Crockett were appointed Youth Leaders. The Crocketts also initiated the Sunday School retreats, using their own van as transportation. Sister Crockett also became the HYPU leader.

The Myles family: Elder Anderson and Sister Mary Myles' children grew up at New Lake. Several moved away at the early age of adulthood. They were: Alberta, Almeter, Fannie Ella, Rosie Bell Anderson, Jr., Carey Samuel, Eddie Lee, Nathaniel and Pearlie Katherine. Reverend and Sister Myles had several grandchildren who were members early in life, before they migrated away from Jackson, MS. Currently three are faithful members; namely Mary Etta Myles Sutton, Robert Earl Myles and Sandrea Jean Myles. Anderson Myles, Jr. and his wife, Armella McNair Myles, their children and some of their grandchildren were part of the youth here at New Lake. Children: Mary Etta Myles Sutton, Robert Earl, Charles Edward, Geraldine Myles Jackson and her children: Ortega, Tawana and Anthony Jackson; Arter Lee, Johnny Nathaniel, his wife Rubye L. Myles and their children, Andrealine Myles Griffin, Sandrea Jean, her son Marcus, her granddaughter, Brianna and Anderson Myles, III. Presently, Ortega Jackson and his wife, Tina Jackson are faithful servants.

Sister Virginia Silas was the first person to serve as the Chair of the New Lake Christian Women Willing Workers (CWWW). The older women at New Lake in those days seemed to have a beautiful, close and cordial relationship. After Sister Silas, several ladies served in succession as president of the Women's Work. Among them Sister Magolia Castilla and Sister Mary J. Thomas was in charge of Standard Bearers and Sunbeams. Others who served as President were: Sisters Armella Myles, Theresa P. Castilla, Pearlie K. Barnes, Daisy Ballard Cobbins, M. Abranese Castilla, Betty Robinson, Jessie M. Williams and Cheryl Coleman. Most of our young females were active in the Sunbeams and Standard Bearers, which were subsidiaries of the CWWW.

During the 1950s, Brother Willenham Castilla was instrumental in organizing a Boys Leadership Club at the church. We fellowshipped and taught leadership principles. Improvement projects such as, installing a gas heater in the sanctuary, planting and cultivating shrubbery on the premises. This was the forerunner of what is now known as the National Brotherhood of the COCHUSA.

MUSIC

The choir has been one of the most spiritual and effective ministries in New Lake Church throughout the years. With great fondness, we remember Deacon Henry Patrick, Deacon Abraham Castilla, Sister Josephine Williams, Sister Magolia Castilla and other sisters including the members of the following: The Silas' the Edgar Williams, the Patrick's and the Myles Brothers which had a quartette that represented New Lake on various occasions and the people came from miles away to hear them sing! History records the men as being praiseworthy for Christ.

Brother Abraham Castilla's greatest love in the church seemed to be the music. He had some training as a vocalist. As parents of the Castillas, he and his wife, Magolia Castilla would sing duets at home and sometimes at church. This was praiseworthy for family and provided spiritual structure growth and development.

Down through the years, the pianists and choirs have been very effective in worship, evangelism and training in the church. Some pianists recalled were: Sister Sally Thomas from Christ Temple, the mother church, Henrene Patrick, Maudell Williams, Jessie Magolia Castilla, Brother J. C. Williams from Cynthia, Brother (later Elder) W. Cortez Castilla, Brother (later Elder) Quemardo M. Castilla, Sisters Trenia Allen and Cherrita Speech, and others who assisted from time to time, including Sister Earnestine Tate Ephfrom and Brother Aaron Thompson.

At this writing (2017), we have five main choirs or singing groups; namely the Voices of Victory, Anointed Praise, the Male Chorus (Might Men), Teenage Choir, and Children's Choir. We have regular instrumental accompaniment in the form of piano, organ, digital keyboard, drums, and bass. Also, several youths play other musical instruments, such as horns, from time to time.

ADDITIONAL MINISTRIES

Other ministries of New Lake under direction of the Parent Body have been and are:

Annual Commemoration and Celebration

1. Church Retreat
2. Pastor Anniversary
3. Call to Harvest
4. Annual Birthday Celebration
5. Homecoming (until 2002)

Children Church Ministry

Christian Education Ministry

Courtesy & Greetings Ministry

Evangelism Team

Food Service & Fellowship Ministry

Library Committee and Etiquette Class

Married Couples Ministry

Media Ministry

Nursery Ministry

Publicity and Public Relations

Usher & Nurses Ministry

Van Ministry

Pastor

Elder Eddie L. Brown, Sr.
Pastor

Deacon Board

Deacon Johnny
Stewart
Chairman

Deacon Michael
Anderson

Deacon Emeritus
Willenham Castilla

Deacon Walter
Crockett

Deacon Herbert
Irvin

Deacon Centron
Lenoir

Deacon Curtis
Proctor

Deacon Thomas G.
Sutton

Church Staff

Sis. Sonya
Parker
Church Clerk

Sis. Courtney
Proctor
Assistant Church
Clerk

Sis. Nancy
Whitehead
Financial Secretary

Sis. Cheryl
Coleman
Assistant Financial
Secretary

Sis. Sandrea
Myles
Treasurer

Sis. Jackie
Hendricks
Assistant Treasurer

Church Boards

Deacon Board

Members of Deacon Board from L-R Deacon Walter
Crockett, Deacon Curtis Proctor, Deacon Willenham
Castilla, Chariman Johnny Stewart, Deacon Herbert
Irvin and Deacon Centron Lenoir Not pictured
Deacons Thomas Sutton and Michael Anderson

Trustee Board

Membersof Trustee Board from L-R Bro.
Robert Myles, Bro. Ollie McClendon, Bro.
Kim Wade and Bro. Lenard Brent Not
Pictured Chairman Alveno Castilla, Bro
Tony Jones and Bro. Portis Perkins

Deaconess Board

Members of Deaconess Board from L-R Sis.
Marlene Cline, Sis. Shirley McClendon,
Sis. Mamie Crockett, Sis. Lurlean Irvin,
Sis. Wanda Bell and Chairlady Earnestine
Ephfrom Not Pictured Sis. Mary Etta Sutton

SOME OF OUR GOALS AND OBJECTIVES

At the end of the year 2009, New Lake sought to increase the Ministry of God benefiting the surrounding community. Over the past 20-25 years, we were blessed to purchase 34 acres of land nearby and five additional acres surrounding the church building. This gave us a total of about 40 acres of land in the city of Jackson. The mortgage of the church, erected in 1988, was burned in 2008.

Currently, plans are to be a major positive force, a beacon, which people can benefit from our presence here on the corner of Livingston and Beasley Roads. The present desire is to provide holistic services for the Lakeover area, Valley North, Richwood, Woodlea and Woodhaven neighborhoods. We believe that our Lord desires the visible church to serve mankind.

New Lake's Mission is *to be the church that loves God with all our hearts, minds and strength; to go with unconditional love, to reach the lost and hurting with the gospel of Jesus Christ; and to make disciples and send them to the uttermost parts of the earth.*

*Come, join us as we are reaching the lost and teaching
the saved to serve as disciples of Jesus Christ.*

OTHER NOTES

This project first began in 2013, and was completed in 2017. It covered the early history of New Lake up until 2009. Since 2009, many changes and developments (including people, events, projects and things) have occurred which, although noteworthy, could not, from a practical standpoint for many reasons, be incorporated or updated into the final product (although several selected updates were made). Accordingly, there may be information that may appear to be inconsistent or out of date, but again, that is a result of the extended time over which this work was completed using volunteer editing efforts. If there are glaring oversights or omissions, please know that that was not the intent of the compiler or the editors.

Various preachers who came to run revivals and other evangelistic services: Elder John Elder, C. C. Carhee, Elder Hence B (Bum) Johnson, Elder George A. Thomas and Elder W.
A. Nolley.

Other preachers who filled in as assistants from time to time on more or less regular basis were: Elder Willie Bingham, Elder D. L. Dyson, Elder M. Horton and Elder (later Bishop) M. D. Bingham.

One very unique occurrence and activity took place in the late 1940s. This was the time when Reverend Yonkers, a Caucasian minister of the Gospel from somewhere in the northern states came into this area to do Bible training, evangelistic and general Christian work, especially among the youth and children. New Lake Church was, at first the only local church that accepted him. Reverend Yonkers was a very effective influence in the general community in a positive way. Many of our young people in the surrounding area experienced Bible Camp, fellowship, witnessing and learned many scriptures during the several years that Reverend Yonkers was introduced to New Lake by the late Sister Laura WillEtta McNair, a nurse for the Yonkers family and the mother of the late Sister Armella McNair Myles.

At this writing, New Lake Church is 111 years old.

We give God the glory for His sustaining love, mercy and grace.

ADDENDUM

The Church of Christ is the Body of Christ (Ephesians 1:22-23; I Corinthians 12; Romans 2:4-5). In this body, as in His human body before His crucifixion, the will of God is done on earth (Hebrews 10: 8-9). In the Church, this work is continued.

Therefore, as a local congregation, New Lake Church is an integral part of the church body, as well as, many charitable and Christian civic activities in the community. This is done prayerfully, physically and financially.

Our national obligations include:

1. The World Mission Board of COCHUSA which has affiliated churches and mission work in West Africa (especially in Liberia); the Dominican Republic and several other locations.
2. The National Publishing Board which publishes and contracts our official literature, manuals, hymnals, etc.
3. The Church Extension-Mission Board –– This board has authority to recommend the acquisition of property, add new congregations and assist evangelistic work.
4. The General Board of Claimants supervises the department of superannuated ministers, missionaries, evangelists, their widows and orphans of the COCHUSA.
5. The NATIONAL Educational ––Trustee Board which operates Christ Missionary and Industrial College, our only institution of learning, which is located in Jackson, Mississippi. It is composed of a Day Care through high school and Bible College. The campus contains 23.6 acres in the city and consists of four buildings. The K- 12 school is accredited by Mississippi Private School Accrediting Association. The Bible College (Department of Religious Education) is accredited by Accrediting Commission International.
6. The Board of Bishops is chiefly supported by their respective dioceses.
7. Other National efforts supported by New Lake are:
    a. The Conic Foundation (Home for the Aged), Jackson, MS
    b. The Master Plan General Campsite, Canton

Some of the local agencies systematically supported by New Lake Church:

1. Center for Pregnancy Choices
2. Educating Africans for Christ
3. Friends of Alcoholics
4. Caring & Sharing School
5. Gateway Rescue Mission Ministries
6. Hope House
7. Salvation Army
8. Stewpot Community Services
9. We Will Go Ministries
10. Forest Avenue Nursing Home

BOOKLETS BY NEW LAKE MEMBERS

Membership Handbook and A Practical Guide for Evangelism

Can be found in their entirety in the

New Lake COCHUSA Library

5907 Livingstion Road

Jackson, MS

601 982-1531

A PRACTICAL GUIDE FOR EVANGELISM

Prepared by
THE NEW LAKE CHURCH EVANGELISM TEAM

New Lake Church of Christ (Holiness) U.S.A.
Livingston Road at Beasley Road
Jackson, Mississippi

A PRACTICAL GUIDE FOR EVANGELISM

Prepared

THE NEW LAKE CHURCH EVANGELISM TEAM
Livingston at Beasly Road

Published

NEW LAKE CHURCH OF CHRIST (HOLINESS) U.S.A.
Jackson and Terry District
South Central Diocese

PASTOR
Rev. Thomas M. Jenkins

Daisy Ballard Cobbins
Editor

July, 1986
Jackson, Mississippi

TABLE OF CONTENTS

New Lake Church Evangelism Team

1986

Membership Handbook
(Revised)

For

New Lake Church
of Christ (Holiness) U.S.A.

Livingston at Beasley Roads

Prepared by

Daisy Ballard Cobbins
and
Marcia Conston

Jackson, Mississippi
1993

TABLE OF CONTENTS

REFERENCES

Information compiled herein has come from several sources. As well as, could be ascertained, all is authentic, primary, secondary and solicited information. Other authorities sources: church record books, yearbooks, interviews, personal recollections and unpublished items.

Castilla, W. 2007. Moving Forward on God's Highway, A Textbook History of the Church of Christ (Holiness) USA, Bloomington, Inc. Author House.

Cobbins, O. B. History of the Church of Christ (Holiness) USA 1895-1065. COCHUSA: National Publishing Board.

Holy Bible, King James Version, Scriptures.

National Publishing Board. Truth Magazine. Bishop Dale Cudjoe, Chief Editor National Publishing Board. 1977. His Fullness Songs. Jackson, MS: Church of Christ (Holiness) USA